THE PENITENT

THE PENITENT

A PLAY BY

David Mamet

THEATRE COMMUNICATIONS GROUP / NEW YORK / 2018

The Penitent is published by Theatre Communications Group, Inc., 520 Eighth Avenue, 24th Floor, New York, NY 10018-4156

The publication of *The Penitent* by David Mamet, through TCG's Book Program, is made possible in part by the New York State Council on the Arts with the support of Governor Andrew Cuomo and the New York State Legislature.

TCG books are exclusively distributed to the book trade by Consortium Book Sales and Distribution.

Library of Congress Control Numbers:
2017051553 (print) / 2017051632 (ebook)
ISBN 978-1-55936-569-7 (paperback) / ISBN 978-1-55936-886-5 (ebook)
A catalog record for this book is available from the Library of Congress.

Book design and composition by Lisa Govan
Cover design by Lisa Govan
Cover photo by Brigitte Lacombe

First Edition, April 2018

THE PENITENT

PRODUCTION HISTORY

The Penitent had its world premiere at the Atlantic Theater Company (Neil Pepe, Artistic Director; Jeffory Lawson, Managing Director) in New York City on February 8, 2017. It was directed by Neil Pepe. The scenic design was by Tim Mackabee, the costume design was by Laura Bauer, the lighting design was by Donald Holder; the production stage manager was Mary Kathryn Flynt. The cast was:

CHARLES	Chris Bauer
KATH	Rebecca Pidgeon
RICHARD	Jordan Lage
AN ATTORNEY	Lawrence Gilliard, Jr.

CHARACTERS

CHARLES, middle-aged man
KATH, Charles's wife, middle-aged woman
RICHARD, their friend
AN ATTORNEY

I was covered with shame and tears for things past, and yet had at the same time a secret surprising joy at the prospect of being a true penitent . . .

—DANIEL DEFOE, *MOLL FLANDERS*

SCENE 1

Charles and Kath.
    At rise, Kath is sitting at a table reading a newspaper.
    Charles enters.

KATH: . . . Richard called. He . . .
CHARLES: Yes, hold on.
KATH: What is it?
CHARLES: Can I sit for a moment?
KATH: Of course.

    (Pause.)

CHARLES: I may need to go away.
KATH: To go away?
CHARLES: Yes.
KATH: Why?
CHARLES: . . . To think this through.

KATH: You need to go away.

CHARLES: Yes.

KATH: Have you discussed it with Richard?

CHARLES: No.

KATH: Then who helped you arrive at this decision?

CHARLES: I came to it on my own.

KATH: With whose help?

CHARLES: It doesn't do any good. To disparage *him* . . .

KATH: It does *me* good.

CHARLES: Yes, all right. Kath. I'd like you to understand.

KATH: Then you're going to have to explain it to me.

CHARLES: I *need*. To . . .

KATH: To "find some solace," is that right?

CHARLES: That's right.

KATH: To "take yourself out of the fray"?

CHARLES: Or: to find some "wisdom."

KATH: Because of the *boy*.

(Pause.)

It started with the boy.

CHARLES: Please . . . ?

KATH: Didn't it? Your "studies . . ."

CHARLES: Yes. That's right.

KATH: . . . that "occupy" you . . .

CHARLES: I've tried to explain it to you.

KATH: Then you must be holding something back. Or else I'm stupid, which may be the case. Or insufficiently "moral."

CHARLES: Neither of which are the case.

KATH: Well, then I don't understand. And Richard needs to speak to you.

CHARLES: *About?*

KATH: . . . the "*Manifesto*" . . . ?

CHARLES: . . . it's just a letter.

KATH: The boy called it that.

CHARLES: He never did. I don't believe he did.

KATH: The *press* did.

CHARLES: That's right.

KATH: He wrote so vilely about you.

CHARLES: I was one of a number on his list.

KATH: Why did they publish it?

CHARLES: I don't know. Because it's scurrilous.

KATH: If they were "out to get you."

CHARLES: And you think they're not?

KATH: Why would they be?

CHARLES: It's human nature.

KATH: What is?

CHARLES: To turn vicious when frightened.

KATH: Is that "wisdom"?

CHARLES: I think it is.

KATH: Why does Richard need to talk to you?

CHARLES: Well, it would be a "legal matter."

KATH: About some "statement"?

CHARLES: What statement?

KATH: I don't know. What is the *legal matter*?

CHARLES *(Gestures)*: It's in the *paper*.

KATH *(Referring to the paper)*: It's about what you wrote?

CHARLES: I never wrote it.

KATH: You didn't write what they said?

CHARLES: Of course not.

KATH: Why of course?

CHARLES: Do you think that's what I ever felt?

KATH: But it's in the paper.

CHARLES: Well, they've taken the side of the boy, then, haven't they?

KATH: Why would they do that?

CHARLES: I told you.

KATH: Tell me again.

CHARLES: Because that's their job.

KATH: After what he did?

CHARLES: Yes.

KATH: I don't understand.

CHARLES: They're in the business of selling papers. To do so, they reduce a horrifying, complex act, to a myth. A myth contains a monster and a victim. Every story needs a victim.

KATH: But the people he killed. They're the victims.

CHARLES: But they're not news. That was last month's news.

KATH: And so, their new victim. Is the boy?

CHARLES: That's right.

KATH: But he's a murderer.

CHARLES: But that's no longer news.

KATH: And so, now *you're* the news?

CHARLES *(Referring to the paper)*: *You* read it.

KATH: I did. But I don't understand.

CHARLES *(Takes the paper)*: "Well-known and marginalized. In professional circles. For referring to homosexuality as an 'aberration.'"

(Pause.)

KATH: And that's why the boy wrote that he hates you?

CHARLES: He hates everyone. He's sick.

KATH: But he hates you for *writing* that? He *read* it?

CHARLES: He could not have read it as I never wrote it.

KATH: That's not what the paper says.

CHARLES: I never wrote it.

KATH: I don't understand.

CHARLES: I never *wrote* it. Do you want the page number? *New Psychiatric Ethics*, page 343. I *wrote*: "Homosexuality Considered As an *Adaptation*." *That's* the title of my paper.

KATH: You never wrote it was an aberration?

CHARLES: *New Psychiatric Ethics*, page 343. "Homosexuality Considered As an *Adaptation*." That's what I . . . Do you want to read the essay?

KATH: And, so what does it mean?

CHARLES: It means they committed libel.

KATH: That the paper did?

CHARLES: That's right.

KATH: They lied about you?

CHARLES: Yes.

KATH: And that constitutes libel?

CHARLES: They lied, they did it knowingly, and it caused me injury.

KATH: Has it?

CHARLES: It will, if it's not rebutted. And it may do so even then.

KATH: Why did they do it?

CHARLES: I told you.

KATH: No. No, you didn't. Why did the paper write it? If it was a lie? Because they're *evil*?

(Pause.)

Charles?

CHARLES: Human nature is evil.

KATH: Well. That's a new view of the world. Isn't it? For a *doctor*? Charles?

CHARLES: No. It's an ancient view. Which we embrace. When we are turned upon. Through no fault of our own . . . When a false *accusation* . . .

KATH: But . . .

CHARLES: And I'd so like you to understand it.

KATH: I . . .

CHARLES: . . . because you're going to share it with me.

KATH: It?

CHARLES: The trauma.

KATH: And so you want me to understand it?

CHARLES: Because I need to protect you.

KATH: Is that what the "rabbi" says?

(Pause.)

CHARLES: *Kath.* I'm being *attacked.*

(Pause.)

Undeservedly. That's true. And greatly troubling. I determined. I needed some wisdom. So I have been speaking with the rabbi.

KATH: And what is the "wisdom"?

CHARLES: The wisdom is in *seeking* wisdom.

KATH: He can't help you with "the law."

CHARLES: No.

KATH: Only with "wisdom" . . . ?

CHARLES: When did you speak to Richard?

KATH: Just now. A while ago.

CHARLES: Was he at his office?

(Charles picks up the phone.)

KATH: . . . at the office? I don't . . .

CHARLES: Did he *call* you?

KATH: He called here, yes.

CHARLES: Al . . .

KATH: Looking for you.

CHARLES *(Hanging up the phone)*: All right, he isn't at the office?

KATH: I don't know where he is.

CHARLES: He . . .

KATH: He said he'd call back.

CHARLES: What does he mean "a statement"?

KATH: They want you to make a statement.

CHARLES: Who?

KATH: The *press*; I . . .

CHARLES: Ab . . . ?

KATH: *I* don't know, about the *boy* . . . ?

CHARLES: Yes, I understand. But, what, what sort of a "statement" can I make? Doesn't he know that? *You* know that.

KATH: I do?

CHARLES: Well, for God's sake, yes. How can I . . . What does he expect that I can "comment" on? For God's . . . what the *hell*, am I *supposed* . . .

KATH: Don't . . .

CHARLES: . . . to . . . *to issue* what? A *disclaimer*?

KATH: Please don't raise your voice at me.

CHARLES: I beg your pardon.

(He picks up the phone and dials again.)

KATH: He said he'd call back.

CHARLES: He'll "call back," because I couldn't reach him?

KATH: All I can tell you are his exact words. And this is all I know. That Richard? Needs to *speak* with you. Regarding "making some sort of . . ."

CHARLES: "On"?

KATH: . . . I don't know. He can't be reached, and he will call you back. That's all he said. You've spoken to the press before.

CHARLES: Never about one of my patients.

KATH: He isn't your patient anymore. Charles?

CHARLES: The rules still appl . . . Why did he call when he knew I'd be out?

KATH: How would he know that?

CHARLES: What time did he call?

KATH: I don't know. An *hour*?

CHARLES: Why would he call me here?

KATH: Why won't you make a statement?

CHARLES: The rules, all right, the rules about prin . . .

KATH: . . . an *hour* ago? I think that's when he called.

(Charles tries the phone again.)

The "rules"?

CHARLES: What?

KATH: The rules? About *privilege*?

CHARLES: About confidentiality, yes.

KATH: Mean that you can't "make a statement"?

CHARLES: Yes.

KATH: Why?

CHARLES: Because the interchange is *protected*. So that the *patient* is protected.

KATH: So . . . ?

CHARLES: So that he's free to speak.

KATH: So then *you* can't reveal "your thoughts"?

CHARLES: Essentially, yes.

KATH: Or what a patient may have said.

CHARLES: That's correct.

KATH: Unless he chooses to have it revealed.

CHARLES: That's right.

KATH: But then he *did* choose to reveal it. The boy. The, the content of your *sessions*.

CHARLES *(Simultaneously with "sessions")*: Who told you that?

KATH: Didn't he?

CHARLES: Did Richard tell you that?

(Pause.)

KATH: Yes.

CHARLES: What else did he say?

KATH: I told you all he said.

CHARLES: Well, hold on. Because *you* said . . .

KATH: I can't remember all he said. He *called* to say you had to speak to him. He said he'd call back. He said perhaps you should make a statement.

CHARLES: I *should* make it? Or that they *requested* it?

KATH: Please don't interrogate me.

CHARLES: Why did he call here?

KATH: Why shouldn't he call here?

CHARLES: All right. I need to talk to him. *When* I've talked to him. Several things will become more clear. Now? I cannot divulge: *confidential information* gained *through* my interchanges with . . .

KATH: Unless it constitutes "danger to oneself or others."

CHARLES: Ah-huh.

KATH: What does that mean?

CHARLES: It means I believe you should not be involved.

KATH: How can I not be involved when I'm your wife?

CHARLES: Then *as* my wife. As difficult as this may be? I *require* . . .

KATH: Require?

CHARLES: You: to stand with me. I have to *navigate* a. A difficult . . . Kath, what you may see as my *reluctance*, or "intransigence," if you will, is not a "lack of trust," but, an obligation. To protect, my pat . . .

KATH: He's not your patient.

CHARLES: He was. And *myself*, and to protect *you*.

KATH: By refusing to talk to me?

CHARLES: That's right.

KATH: And that will somehow "protect" me?

CHARLES: Yes. It will.

KATH: I *told* you. It would come to this . . . because I *saw*. And you said I was a fool.

CHARLES: I never sss . . .

KATH: I *told* you. And you wouldn't listen.

CHARLES: . . . and I . . .

KATH: At the time I *told* you. *At the very time.* That you should speak to the *press.*

CHARLES: What do you think I should have told them?

KATH: . . . which refusal . . .

CHARLES: . . . what . . . ?

KATH: *Predictably infuriated* . . .

CHARLES: What could I . . . ?

KATH: You could have expressed: *sorrow*, you . . .

CHARLES: He was my patient. I could *not*, by my oath, comment on his *treatment.* And, it was deemed *inappropriate.* For me. To express sorrow. For the victims.

KATH: How could that have been inappropriate?

CHARLES: As it could have been seen as a violation of my oath.

KATH: Why?

CHARLES: As *Richard* said, as an indictment of an act *allegedly* committed by a patient in my care.

KATH: I don't understand.

CHARLES: *Listen* to me: in what *capacity*. All right? Would I comment on the act of a patient *under my* care, who was "presumed innocent"?

KATH: . . . I . . .

CHARLES: My *comment*, wait, could only have been taken as acknowledgment of his guilt.

KATH: You couldn't express sorrow that those people died?

CHARLES: In what capacity?

KATH: But it's absurd.

CHARLES: I agree with you. But I was *advised*. And I took the advice.

KATH (*Referring to the paper*): And now they've found *this*: "Homosexuality as an aberration . . ."

CHARLES: It's a lie. And easily disproved.

KATH: And the boy wrote that you hate him. Because he was gay.

(Pause.)

In his letter.

CHARLES: That's what he wrote of *everyone*. Didn't you *read* it?

KATH: . . . but.

CHARLES: It's a *lie*. Don't you know it's a lie?

KATH: Yes, but he *wrote* it. That you wouldn't *help* him. Because he was gay. Charles?

CHARLES: That he wrote it. Does not make it true. *You* know what the boy is.

KATH: What is he?

CHARLES: He's a psychopath. And he's a murderer. And his "letter" . . . his "letter" . . . his "*Manifesto*" . . .

KATH: But, now, he's the victim?

CHARLES: That's right.

KATH: Why?

CHARLES: Because they must have a new villain.

KATH: Who?

CHARLES: His defense. And the press.

KATH: They need a new villain?

CHARLES: Yes.

KATH: So now it's not the boy.

CHARLES: That's right.

KATH: It's *you.*

CHARLES: That's right. It's me.

SCENE 2

Charles and Richard.

CHARLES: Tell me about the libel case.

RICHARD: They agree it was a copy editor's mistake.

CHARLES: *Really.*

RICHARD: And they'll print a retraction.

CHARLES: The paper will print a retraction.

RICHARD: That's right.

CHARLES: No, it's not enough.

RICHARD: I'd advise you to accept it.

CHARLES: Some disclaimer at the bottom of page twelve.

RICHARD: That's right.

CHARLES: And they've destroyed my *reputation*.

RICHARD: They're a newspaper, that's what they do. D'you ever read them?

CHARLES: But it's libel.

RICHARD: We would have to demonstrate malice.

CHARLES: What does that mean?

RICHARD: Intent to harm. Or reckless disregard. They'll say it was simply a misprint.

CHARLES: "Homosexuality as an *aberration*"? I wrote "*adaptation*." Hardly similar words. And that's a misprint?

RICHARD: Yes.

CHARLES: *Without* evil intent?

RICHARD: Perhaps it was an unconscious . . .

CHARLES: I don't . . .

RICHARD: The copy editor, for example, they'd suggest, might have been "uneasy with the concept."

CHARLES: . . . yes?

RICHARD: Of homosexuality. It might be a simple "Freudian slip," or . . .

CHARLES: You believe that?

RICHARD: A jury might.

CHARLES: It's absurd.

RICHARD: I understand. But a jury might accept it. The paper? *Their* bet is: Do you want to go to court, against their battery of lawyers, and unlimited wealth, and have them drag it out forever? Or . . .

CHARLES: . . . They libeled me . . .

RICHARD: *Or*: Are you willing to accept the fiction they intended no harm, call it a draw, and walk away.

CHARLES: And what do I gain?

RICHARD: You'll have acknowledged their power and, so, stilled their enmity.

CHARLES: But they attacked *me*.

RICHARD: They're in that business. Charles? That's what they do. You do not, as the man said, pick a fight with someone who buys ink by the carload. You take their apology, it's cocktail chat for two weeks. It's a silly mistake, and you're done. If you *oppose* them, you'll be their new animal to torture. And you'll be on the front page till the end of time. Accept their apology, and let it die. It's good advice.

CHARLES: Whoever took good advice?

RICHARD: You be the first.

(Pause.)

CHARLES: All right. Yes, I will.

(Pause.)

Thank you.

RICHARD: You're welcome. And you agree to testify. For the defense.

CHARLES: What?

RICHARD: No, you heard me.

CHARLES: I won't testify for him.

(Pause.)

I won't testify for the boy.

RICHARD: You wouldn't be testifying "for the boy." You'd be testifying for "the defense."

CHARLES: Oh, really.

RICHARD: Yes. It's a legal fiction—it's known as "the law."

CHARLES: No, please don't lecture me.

RICHARD: It will help get you off the front page.

CHARLES: Will it indeed?

RICHARD: Yes.

CHARLES: How?

RICHARD: It will establish your bona fides.

CHARLES: Which were in doubt because . . . ?

RICHARD: What does it matter?

(Pause.)

CHARLES: No. I won't testify.

RICHARD: Charles? You *need*. To "surrender." Is that a "blow to your pride"? Yes? I understand. Is it worth it? I think it *is*. Look, this is a loathsome business. The Law. As is Journalism, and Medicine, for all I know. And my job. Is to help you through it. Whatever your, understandable distress, or rage, or doubts . . .

CHARLES: About?

RICHARD: Well . . .

CHARLES: My doubts about *what*?

RICHARD: . . . your *treatment*, perhaps, your treatment of the boy. *I* don't know . . . Your . . .

CHARLES: Do I have doubts about "my treatment" . . . ?

RICHARD: The boy. Under your care. Committed a crime. That must feel dreadful.

CHARLES: Yes. It does.

RICHARD: I'm sure it does. But the boy. Though he was in your care. Was not in your control. Isn't that right? *Isn't* it?

CHARLES: Yes. That's right.

RICHARD: He was acting. Independent of you. And in *spite* of whatever aid, or treatment, or "direction" you might have given him. In *spite* of it. Not *because* of it.

(Pause.)

CHARLES: That's correct.

RICHARD: He was out of control.

CHARLES: I . . .

RICHARD: . . . he was out of *your* control.

CHARLES: That's right.

RICHARD: That's all they're going to ask you. On the stand. "Is it not possible *his* actions were those over which he had no control?" It's called the "benefit of the doubt." Is it *impossible* his actions were the result of conditions over which he had no control?

CHARLES: How the hell would *I* know?

RICHARD: You just *told* me that's the case. The history is clear.

CHARLES: No one wants the history. They want a case made for the defense.

RICHARD: And can you not in conscience make that case? Isn't that the case for psychiatry? Wouldn't you testify? For that? That the boy suffered? *Obviously* he suffered. He came to you. You *treated* him.

CHARLES: I don't know *what* I did for him. I listened to him. I made notes. I said, "What does that make you think of." That's what analysis *is*. It *is* "nonintervention."

RICHARD: And, so, it's not "treatment"?

CHARLES: How did I "treat him"? His "mental illness."

RICHARD: And then, what is *mental illness*?

CHARLES: I don't know. It's a "disruption of the spirit."

RICHARD: But that's just giving it another name.

CHARLES: Yes. That's right. And it's doing something else.

RICHARD: Which is?

CHARLES: It's a "confession of humility."

(Pause.)

RICHARD: You've testified before.

CHARLES: I did.

(Pause.)

RICHARD: They'll turn on you.

CHARLES: I don't know but that I don't deserve it.

RICHARD: Well. I know you're *hurt*. You've been shocked. And I think you've been brutalized. And you're confused. And angry. All I can offer you is legal advice. Which is, I swear to you, best calculated to relieve the legal portion of your burden.

(Pause.)

Agree to their retraction. This is the best advice you'll ever have. Let it blow over, and it will.

CHARLES: And if it doesn't?

RICHARD: We're talking about a suit for damages. My advice is based upon the *legal* merits. Of the suit. I advise you, *strongly*, *not* to pursue it.

CHARLES: I agree to accept their apology?

RICHARD: They'll say *correction*. And we're done.

(Pause.)

CHARLES: All right.

RICHARD: You agree, it was a regrettable misprint. *With*, of course, no intent to malign.

CHARLES: All right.

RICHARD: And that the case, *itself* is a tragedy. For all concerned.

CHARLES: I don't understand.

RICHARD: *Isn't* it?

CHARLES: No; *where*, where do I agree to that?

RICHARD: In your statement. In their paper.

CHARLES: Wait. They want *me*. To make a statement. *In their newspaper*. Clearing *them*? Is *that* what they're offering?

RICHARD: They're *offering* you: space in which to make a statement. You may use it to clear *them* and to clear *yourself*. That's their apology.

CHARLES: To "clear myself"?

RICHARD: Yes.

CHARLES: Of *what?*

(Pause.)

No. I won't do it.

SCENE 3

Charles and Kath.

KATH: But I don't understand it.

CHARLES: Do you want me to tell you again?

KATH: Richard said . . .

CHARLES: When did you see Rich . . . ?

KATH: He told me the "facts."

CHARLES: . . . the *"facts."*

KATH: I understand the "facts." But I can't understand what you're doing.

CHARLES: When did you see Richard?

KATH: Why should I not see him?

CHARLES: It's not, Kath. I beg your pardon. That you shouldn't *see* him. But, I assume, it was in connection with the case.

KATH: I . . .

CHARLES: Or that you discussed the case.

KATH: Why should we not discuss the case?

CHARLES: Be . . .

KATH: What else have I to discuss?

   (Simultaneously) Do you think it was dis . . .

CHARLES *(Simultaneously)*: I . . . no, I'm sorry, go on.

(Pause.)

Go on.

KATH: Did you think it was "disloyal"? To discuss the case with him?

CHARLES: I . . . I don't *know*.

KATH: Well. He's the only . . . Now? He's the only person I *can* talk to, without . . .

CHARLES: Apart from me . . .

KATH: Either, all right, encountering *scorn* . . .

CHARLES: . . . yes . . .

KATH: Or . . .

CHARLES: Or pity?

KATH: Yes, or "pity."

CHARLES: . . . for living with *me*.

KATH: Yes, pity for living with you, I'm sorry. *I* don't feel it. *I* . . .

CHARLES: What do you feel?

KATH: I'm *confused*. As there are those, not friends, not close friends, but "acquaintances" or . . . Yes. *Or* friends, who, you see, cannot decide . . .

CHARLES: Yes? . . . Who . . . ?

KATH: When they see me. If they see me on the *street*, or . . . Because, where can they go?

(Pause.)

When they see me.

CHARLES: I'm sorry.

KATH: Or decide. Whether to *talk* to me. Perhaps you know; I think, though, that you *don't* know. Because . . .

CHARLES: . . . I'm sure.

KATH: Because it's *your* choice. So perhaps you can *live* with it. It's not *my* choice. You, at least have the satisfaction . . .

CHARLES: . . . Kath.

KATH: Of what, of "standing up" . . . of "standing up for . . ."

CHARLES: Yes.

KATH: . . . if *that's* . . . But *other* people. Might *wonder*, you see . . .

CHARLES: Yes.

KATH: Or "cross the room."

CHARLES: I understand.

KATH: As if I didn't see them. And *wonder*. About *my* loyalties.

CHARLES: And, you'd be forgiven . . .

KATH: For?

CHARLES: For being torn. By feelings of disloyalty. If that's what you feel?

KATH: I don't know what I feel.

(Pause.)

CHARLES: I've always treasured. Above all things.

(Pause.)

KATH: What?

CHARLES: Your loyalty.

KATH: . . . No.

CHARLES: But I understand, yes, I have. Kath. You're intensely loyal.

KATH: I don't think so.

CHARLES: No, it doesn't mean "without doubts" . . .

KATH: Well, that's me.

CHARLES: Or "without regrets."

KATH: It doesn't mean "without regrets"?

CHARLES: No. It means "loyal in *actions*."

(Pause.)

KATH: But I have disloyal thoughts.

CHARLES: Of course you do. Everyone does.

KATH: *You* don't.

CHARLES: I'm sure that I do.

KATH: No. You're better than I.

CHARLES: Hardly.

KATH: Of course you are. How can you say you're not? Your, your, your behavior in the *case*.

CHARLES: "The case." How is that *loyalty*?

KATH: *I* don't know.

CHARLES: But you said it was "loyalty."

KATH: You're loyal to your "Oath."

CHARLES: Is that how you understand it?

KATH: Am I wrong?

CHARLES: But I'm not loyal to *you*? . . . That's what you feel? Is that right?

KATH: I don't know what I feel.

CHARLES: Because I *put* you here. You didn't sign on for . . .

KATH: . . . I married you . . .

CHARLES: This "beating . . ."

KATH: That's true.

CHARLES: Of course it's true.

(Pause.)

KATH: I'm *not sure*. That I *believe* in . . .

CHARLES: . . . in me?

KATH: In what you're doing.

(Pause.)

CHARLES: Is that disloyalty?

KATH: And the people that I see, for *none* of them are neutral . . . how can they be neutral?

CHARLES: People can withhold judgment.

KATH: *Show* them to me. Charles, because *I* haven't seen them. And I doubt that they exist. Because they . . .

CHARLES: . . . There is . . .

KATH: . . . wait. *They*. Our "friends," our . . .

CHARLES: . . . all right.

KATH: *They* have to live.

CHARLES: . . . with you . . .

KATH: No. With each other. And so they have to choose. How to treat me. And it's driving me mad.

CHARLES: Kath . . .

KATH: I can't . . . when the *phone* rings. I pray it's a wrong number. Or a telephone solicitor, or . . .

CHARLES: . . . I'm so sorry.

KATH: Someone who . . . someone . . .

CHARLES: Who doesn't know who you are.

KATH: Who, no, who doesn't know who *you* are. I'm sorry. I don't even know what I'm apologizing for, but I can't . . . I . . .

(Pause.)

CHARLES: How can I help?

KATH: You can't help.

CHARLES: Would you like me to explain it again?

KATH: No, I understand it. I think maybe I understand it. I just hate it.

CHARLES: What would you like me to do?

KATH: I . . . Charles. You're so much more intelligent . . .

CHARLES: . . . that's not true.

KATH: And . . . You tell me, that it's a question of "morality." But *I* don't understand it. Abstractly . . .

CHARLES: I . . .

KATH: But. *But* . . .

(Pause.)

And you're so "good."

CHARLES: Am I good?

KATH: Better than I.

CHARLES: Hardly.

KATH: No. You talk about your "oath." I don't even understand what an "oath" is.

CHARLES: You know what an oath . . . You're saying. Of course you understand the nature of— You married me, you . . .

KATH: Wait, Charles.

CHARLES: You took *that* oath and kept it; and you're a perfect wife . . .

KATH: No, I'm not perfect.

CHARLES: You're *human*. We're all human, of course, and . . .

KATH: Charles.

CHARLES: . . . one, one aspect of intimacy is that: It tests us. In . . . it proves us. In the old sense. It exposes us to *trauma*. We have taken an oath, and, so, when *tempted* . . .

KATH: I can't walk down the street, Charles, or pick up a newspaper. Without seeing your name.

CHARLES: At some point. It will be over.

KATH: I don't see it.

CHARLES: After the trial.

KATH: How will it be over? Who will be my friends?

CHARLES: . . . you'd lose your friends? . . .

KATH: I *have* . . .

CHARLES: But you've done nothing.

KATH: I *know* I've done nothing. But whatever I do . . .

CHARLES: You feel whatever you do is wrong.

KATH: No. I *know* it's wrong.

CHARLES: Because you feel that you're disloyal. And everyone shuns you. Because of me. And to wish for their acceptance is disloyalty. And you've done nothing wrong. Except to marry me. And be a good wife. And now you're being punished. And have thoughts of abandoning me. Is that correct? That might be correct, Kath? But they're just thoughts.

KATH: I don't know that you're right. In what you're doing.

CHARLES: Is it enough. That *I* know what I'm doing is right?

(Pause.)

All right. Then, the question is: "Who can advise you?" Where can you go for help. All these years. You came to me. As I did to *you*. And now you can't come to me in this, because, to *you*, I am the *cause* of your . . . Your trauma.

KATH: Yes. That's right.

CHARLES: No, that's a terrible position.

KATH: Yes. It is.

(Pause.)

CHARLES: You saw Richard.

KATH: Would you prefer I didn't see him?

CHARLES: I would *prefer* you do those things which bring you comfort.

KATH: Do you mean it?

CHARLES: I would do anything. To comfort you.

KATH: Then drop all this fucking nonsense. Drop it. *Make* your statement . . . Go to the court. *Say* what they want, give them whatever they want.

CHARLES: I can't do that.

KATH: Why not?

CHARLES: They might, they might demand the *records*. They . . .

KATH: Why shouldn't you give them the records?

CHARLES: Because they'll just keep escalating their *demands*. *First* . . .

KATH: Give them the records. Why couldn't you give up the records?

CHARLES: *Because they're confidential*. Or else *anyone* . . .

KATH: . . . I . . .

CHARLES: The boy . . .

KATH: I don't care about the boy . . .

CHARLES: Whatever he may have done. He came to me for help. With the understanding. That our interchanges would be priv—

KATH: I don't *care* about the boy. Didn't you *hear* me? He's nothing to me, and he's nothing to *you* . . . And there's nothing you can do for him.

CHARLES: I . . .

KATH: But, I'm your *wife*, Charles? Can you cure *my* suffering? Because I *don't* understand. I only know that I can't take any more. Because I *don't* understand. *You* understand. I envy you.

CHARLES: I'm so sorry, Kath.

KATH: And I wish I could pray. Like you. But I don't know what to pray for.

CHARLES: You could pray in any case.

KATH: And I'm a sinner.

CHARLES: You're the best person I know.

KATH: Is that what your rabbi would say?

CHARLES: Yes. He might.

KATH: How would he know? *He* doesn't know me. All that *I* know: the boy? Of all of us, is the only one who might find peace. Maybe he was *always* in a state of peace. It was only those whose lives he touched that he destroyed.

CHARLES: How can I help you?

KATH: I told you. But you won't do it.

CHARLES: I'm doing what I think is right.

KATH: And I can't leave the house.

CHARLES: What would you like me to do?

KATH: What difference does it make?

SCENE 4

Charles and Richard.

CHARLES: The patient, the patient tells you things. Can you unhear them? No. And as much as your interest may be in a pathology, still, they inform you, *morally* about the human being; *(Pause)* and may awaken prejudices.

RICHARD: No, I asked you a question, Charles. Do you remember what I asked? It could be answered "yes" or "no." You need to keep your answers *short*. To "yes" or "no" if possible.

CHARLES: Yes. You said.

RICHARD: Let's start again . . . "The analyst may form opinions."

CHARLES: That's right.

RICHARD: "But is trained not to act upon, or, differently, to *suppress* them in the interest of aiding the patient."

CHARLES: That's incomplete, but, yes, that's correct.

RICHARD: ". . . you took an oath."

CHARLES: I did.

RICHARD: "As a physician . . . to care for the suffering. And never to *reveal* . . ."

CHARLES: That's right.

RICHARD: "Those secrets which . . ."

CHARLES: You know, I often wondered who the injured person was.

RICHARD: You find this process interesting? Charles? It will be much less interesting on the stand.

CHARLES: No, I know.

RICHARD: No, you *don't* know: a deposition is a fishing trip. No case was ever won in a deposition. Many were lost. Let's practice. Answer the questions, as you'll have to, *yes*.
Or no. "The injured person" . . .

CHARLES: . . . I'm not speaking about the child's *act* . . . I'm . . .

RICHARD: Is the accused a child?

CHARLES: The young man.

RICHARD: But you just called him a child.

CHARLES: He's not a child.

RICHARD: In his mind?

CHARLES: "In his mind." Yes.

RICHARD: "Is that a medical opinion, Doctor?" You see? You make a random comment. And they'll employ it to take you apart. The *smarter* a man is—the easier it is for opposing council to destroy him. Charles? You can't fool a stupid man. The smart man? Will find provocative opportunities for discourse and the other fellow will use them to make him seem a fool. The only way. To control it, is to answer Yes. Or. No.

CHARLES: And that's what it all comes down to?

RICHARD: That's right.

CHARLES: All of my thoughts about "treatment."

RICHARD: Answer yes or no.

CHARLES: All my supposed "training"? A young man. *Suffering.* Came to me for help . . .

RICHARD: Then why don't you help him?

CHARLES: Why didn't I help him?

RICHARD: No. Why *don't* you help him? Now?

CHARLES: By testifying. For him?

RICHARD: Yes. And be done with it.

(Pause.)

CHARLES: I'm tired.

RICHARD: You'll be tired at the deposition.

CHARLES: You know, they *train* you. Or they used to. To function when you're tired. You'd be on a three-day rotation. You were so tired. But you still had to make decisions. It gave you confidence. But it's inevitable. That one makes bad . . .

RICHARD: They may ask . . .

CHARLES: . . . sometimes . . . makes bad decisions . . . I'm sorry?

RICHARD: They may ask do you know: Why did he do it?

CHARLES: Why does anyone do *anything*? Because they *want* to. Have I missed something?

(Pause.)

RICHARD: Off the record?

CHARLES: All right.

RICHARD: Do you believe in psychiatry?

CHARLES: I believe that any professional bears the shame of the questionable worth of his ministrations. I know of my racket what you know of yours: that, for the most part, we are paid for the ability to keep a straight face. While accomplishing little or nothing.

RICHARD: Yes. That's right.

CHARLES: Two sides hire two opposing whores to testify. The jury picks the fellow in the better-cut suit.

RICHARD: That's what the legal process is. That's all it ever was. What else could it be?

(Pause.)

CHARLES: She's so concerned about me.

RICHARD: As she should be.

CHARLES: And you said you could *help* her.

RICHARD: As a friend.

CHARLES: But *how* could you help her?

RICHARD: I could talk to her.

CHARLES: But: you couldn't tell her *everything*.

RICHARD: Ev . . . ?

CHARLES: About the *case*.

RICHARD: Of course not. No.

CHARLES: Because?

RICHARD: You know why.

CHARLES: Our communications? Are privileged.

RICHARD: Yes.

CHARLES: As were mine with the boy. And yet they want me to divulge them.

RICHARD: But you could not help the boy unless *he* told *you* everything.

CHARLES: And "how can you protect me if I cannot tell you 'everything'"?

RICHARD: That's right.

CHARLES: But I took an oath. And. If I "tell you everything," what is to prevent "the law" from extorting, from you the same confidential information, which it wants from *me*? Or, or actually seizing my files?

RICHARD: They might take the files.

CHARLES: What?

RICHARD: They . . .

CHARLES: I don't understand.

RICHARD: They . . .

CHARLES: . . . but they're protected. By law.

RICHARD: It would be tried in court.

CHARLES: Tried? When?

RICHARD: If they subpoenaed them.

CHARLES: You're telling me, that if the government came in and demanded my, confidential records, they might end up in court? The *files*?

RICHARD: They might.

CHARLES: . . . and you don't see that's an outrage?

RICHARD: All right, yes, it's an outrage. What do you wanna do?

(Pause.)

CHARLES: What if they were lost, the *records*?

RICHARD: You don't want to do that.

CHARLES: No. I'm not saying I *would*, but . . .

RICHARD: . . . why, why would you consider that?

CHARLES: . . . as an "act of conscience"? If the government . . .

RICHARD: . . . an act of conscience. But there'd be a penalty.

CHARLES: . . . for?

RICHARD: Obstruction of justice. If you, if *someone* . . .

CHARLES: No, no. I'm saying, if *before* they were requested, if the files were lost . . .

RICHARD: Wait, wait. Stop.

(Pause.)

They'd put you on the stand, and you'd either have to acknowledge your act or commit perjury. Either of which choices would send you to jail . . .

(Pause.)

CHARLES: You said if I made "the statement" I'd be done.

RICHARD: I was wrong. I'm doing the best I can.

CHARLES: And so it never ends. And they'll torture me. Till they've convicted me of something. In the *public mind*. Or driven me mad, or . . .

RICHARD: . . . I'm sorry.

CHARLES: . . . me or my wife.

RICHARD: How is she?

CHARLES: . . . because of a misprint.

RICHARD: How is Kath?

CHARLES: Not well.

RICHARD: You may have to give up the files.

(Pause.)

Charles, you may . . .

CHARLES: No, I heard you. Thank you.

SCENE 5

Charles and Kath.

KATH: Tell me again.

CHARLES: They may subpoena my records.

KATH: What does Richard say?

CHARLES: That's what he says.

KATH: Can they?

CHARLES: He thinks they can.

KATH: All right. They'd take the *records* to show . . . ?

CHARLES: To show, my . . . my . . .

KATH: Your . . . ?

CHARLES: State of mind.

KATH: *Your* state of mind, *your* . . . ?

CHARLES: Yes. To show prejudice, or . . .

KATH: I . . .

CHARLES: Against the *boy* . . .

KATH: That you were *prejudiced* against him.

CHARLES: Yes.

KATH: *Why?*

CHARLES: Because he's gay.

KATH: But you never said that.

CHARLES: No.

KATH: But *he* said that.

CHARLES: That's right.

KATH: In his "letter."

CHARLES: Yes.

KATH: And you *never* wrote that it was an "aberration."

CHARLES: That's right. But they think, or they pretend to think, in my files, they may find something I *said*, which . . .

KATH: Why are they doing it?

CHARLES: Someone suggested that they could revert to savagery and call it the pursuit of justice. That is the definition of a mob.

KATH: I can't accept that.

CHARLES: No? Then you tell *me* why they're doing it.

KATH: Give up the files.

CHARLES: I can't.

KATH: Well, yes, you "can."

CHARLES: I have to fight for them.

KATH: Why?

CHARLES: Because I took an oath?

KATH: *Ah*-huh.

CHARLES: *Yes.* That's right.

(Pause.)

KATH: Are they going to "win"?

CHARLES: It makes no difference. Do you understand? Or there's no end for me. For *me*, or for any *physician* . . .

KATH: You're not *thinking*.

CHARLES: I've . . . They keep *escalating their demands*. Into an inquisit . . .

KATH: But . . .

CHARLES: They're trying to *destroy* me. It's nothing I've *done*, they . . . ?

KATH: I don't underst . . .

CHARLES: I've *explained* it to you.

KATH: Explain it to me again. I'm stupid.

CHARLES: I don't think you're stupid.

KATH: Well, I fucking must be stupid, 'cause the whole thing is a mystery to me.

CHARLES: They're trying to divert attention from the boy.

KATH: But at some point it has to stop.

CHARLES: He still has to stand trial. Yes.

KATH: So *let* him and let them *try* him. And go along. In *whatever* way they tell you. Doing *whatever* they ask. For as long as it lasts. To *let* them. Do whatever they like. To the boy, who . . .

CHARLES: I know that you think I'm a fool.

KATH: I don't think you're a . . .

CHARLES: But. I. Have. To *make a stand. Somewhere.* I . . .

KATH: *Why?*

CHARLES: Or else. It'll never stop. See what they've done now?

KATH: What have they done now, Charles?

CHARLES: Richard hasn't told you?

KATH: What have they done?

(Pause.)

CHARLES: It seems. They're suggesting my refusal to cooperate may be a violation of his *civil rights*.

KATH: Who is?

CHARLES: The defense.

KATH: Oh no.

CHARLES: Yes.

KATH: Wait.

(Pause.)

Because he's gay . . . ?

CHARLES: . . . which Richard says is a brilliant move on the part of his defense.

KATH: And what does Richard say you should do?

CHARLES: Richard can't help me.

KATH: Who can help you?

CHARLES: I *won't testify for the* . . .

KATH: I *understand.* I *understand* that, but *I don't understand why.*

CHARLES: YOU DON'T HAVE TO UNDERSTAND IT, YOU JUST HAVE TO ACCEPT . . . CAN'T YOU STAND WITH ME, FOR THE LOVE OF GOD?

KATH: Don't *you* fucking scream at me. *I'm* not your adversary. I'm just . . . I'm just . . . Call them up now, and tell them, that you . . .

CHARLES: That I'll "what"?

KATH: That you'll do whatever they ask.

CHARLES: It's too late.

KATH: That you've had a "change of heart," or . . .

CHARLES: I said it's *too fucking late.*

KATH: Or that your "rabbi . . ." I don't give a damn . . .

CHARLES: I can't do it.

KATH: Why can't you do it?

CHARLES: What does it "matter," why? If you won't list . . .

KATH: Please.

CHARLES: Because it's an *inquisition.*

KATH: That's a religious term . . .

CHARLES: . . . and to give into it is *immoral*.

KATH: Which means they want you to "defy the Word of God"?

CHARLES: All right, yes.

KATH: Did you tell them that? Charles . . . ? Did you tell them that? . . .

SCENE 6

Charles and an Attorney.

ATTORNEY: Now, I'd like to ask you about religion.
CHARLES: All right.
ATTORNEY: You call yourself a religious man?
CHARLES: I would.
ATTORNEY: Would you call yourself a zealot?
CHARLES: A zealot. No.
ATTORNEY: A zealot being one inspired by zeal.
CHARLES: . . . I wouldn't think so.
ATTORNEY: You do not feel yourself "inspired by zeal"?
CHARLES: I . . .
ATTORNEY: You find yourself *inspired*?
CHARLES: Perhaps. Sometimes.
ATTORNEY: By what?
CHARLES: Perhaps by *love*.

ATTORNEY: The love of God.

CHARLES: All right.

ATTORNEY: And how do you know God? How does one know God?

CHARLES: Through God's *word*, through . . .

ATTORNEY: You feel inspired by the Word of God.

CHARLES: I do.

ATTORNEY: Do you believe the Bible is the Word of God?

CHARLES: I don't know.

ATTORNEY: You don't know if it's the Word of God.

CHARLES: That's right.

ATTORNEY: But you feel "inspired" by it.

CHARLES: I do.

ATTORNEY: And you've testified you read it daily.

CHARLES: I also read the newspaper.

ATTORNEY: Is it the Word of God? The Bible?

CHARLES: I don't know.

ATTORNEY: But you "believe" in it.

CHARLES: I study to understand it.

ATTORNEY: And those passages you may not understand. There must be passages that you don't understand? . . .

CHARLES: There are.

ATTORNEY: How do you treat them?

CHARLES: I . . .

ATTORNEY: Or say, those passages which you might find objectionable. Are there such passages?

CHARLES: There are those I find disquieting.

ATTORNEY: As, for example?

(*Pause.*)

CHARLES: Nadab and Abihu.

ATTORNEY: Nadab and Abihu. The sons of Aaron.

CHARLES: Very good.

ATTORNEY: Their story is?

CHARLES: They offered up "strange fire" with their prayers. And were slain.

ATTORNEY: For their *impertinence*. In *disobeying* the Word of God?

CHARLES: Perhaps.

ATTORNEY: Or for *interpreting* the Word of God?

CHARLES: Perhaps.

ATTORNEY: The Israelites were directed by God to offer incense in a certain way. Nadab and Abihu improvised or embellished God's instruction. And the Torah says they were consumed by fire. And as a *rational man*. You say you found this disquieting. The Bible lesson: "Do exactly as God says or perish."

(Pause.)

Is that the lesson?

CHARLES: The Bible, may be understood as the Constitution of the Jewish Faith. And there are . . .

ATTORNEY: The Constitution.

CHARLES: And there are three thousand years' worth of *amendments* or "clarifications." The Midrash, the Talmud, *Kabbalah* . . .

ATTORNEY: When did you begin your studies?

CHARLES: Is it pertinent?

ATTORNEY: Well, we'll see . . . But the lesson here is that Nadab and Abihu brought interpretation, or, say, *reason* to these Commandments of God. And so were consumed. It's quite a cautionary tale. Is it not? To those who might consider questioning God's Will. Is that what you learn from the Bible?

CHARLES: I've said, the Torah . . .

ATTORNEY: Is that what you have learned?

CHARLES: Has been continually *amended* . . .

ATTORNEY: Do . . .

CHARLES: Our Supreme Court once ruled that blacks were slaves, and must, if captured, in the North, be returned to their slave masters.

ATTORNEY: Do you believe the Bible is the Word of God?

CHARLES: I believe, at the least, it is *divinely inspired.*

ATTORNEY: How does that differ from "the Word of God. Which must be obeyed"?

CHARLES: The works of Chopin are divinely inspired. Who would deny it? The works of Michelangelo, the . . . If we say, as we do, they are divinely inspired, if all great art is so, are we debarred from saying it of the Bible? What is the difference?

ATTORNEY: Works of art do not carry instructions and prohibitions.

CHARLES: . . . If . . .

ATTORNEY: What is the lesson you would take from the story. Of Nadab and Abihu?

CHARLES: There are many lessons to be . . .

ATTORNEY: What is the lesson for you *now*? In the *tale* of these two men? Who dared to "interpret" the Word of God and were slain for their presumption?

CHARLES: Am I to be persecuted because of my *religious beliefs*?

ATTORNEY: Why, if they are your beliefs, should you be reluctant to announce them?

CHARLES: Shouldn't that be between myself and God?

ATTORNEY: Indeed. Where they *concern* God. But where they concern other men? Who have the right, according to *our* law to demand from you a certain standard of conduct? You, in your profession, delve into men's, men's motivation. Is *that* fair?

CHARLES: Yes. I think it is.

ATTORNEY: Now, you have often. In the past, testified as to the motivation of defendants.

CHARLES: That's correct.

ATTORNEY: Why?

CHARLES: As . . .

ATTORNEY: Yes? Please?

CHARLES: As I believe them entitled to defense.

ATTORNEY: And you believed these defendants' motivation, or "states of mind," might, through your testimony, *mitigate* a legal penalty. Is that correct?

CHARLES: I testified as I thought right.

ATTORNEY: Of course. But you were paid to testify. To your opinion.

CHARLES: Yes. I was paid.

ATTORNEY: And you examined these patients. Prior to sharing your opinion.

CHARLES: Of course.

ATTORNEY: But the *opinion*, of course, was determined prior to the examination.

CHARLES: No. It was not.

ATTORNEY: It was *not*? . . .

CHARLES: No.

ATTORNEY: You have testified in . . . I've noted the number of cases . . . For the *defense*.

CHARLES: . . . Yes . . .

ATTORNEY: . . . You being paid to render an opinion calculated to exculpate the defendant.

CHARLES: No. That was not my calculation. I'm a *doctor*. My job . . .

ATTORNEY: Yes, but your "job" which we may define as a specific *service* you were paid to perform, and which you *did* perform. "For a valuable consideration." Was "to get the defendant off." That's blunt, but it's fair. Isn't it?

CHARLES: We have an adversary legal system. *Some* countries have cases presented to a judge, appointed to rule.

ATTORNEY: . . . We . . .

CHARLES: "In service of the truth." Our system pits two opponents one against the other. Each has a plausible interpretation of the facts. The more persuasive one prevails.

ATTORNEY: Exactly. *Your* job, then, in your testimony for the defense was to offer this "plausible explanation" of facts which would favor the defendant. Or you would not have been engaged. That's logical, isn't it? Or they would have engaged someone else.

CHARLES: All right.

ATTORNEY: *However*, you might have felt about the defendant, or his alleged crime. Yes, we, in court, are *bound* to consider the defendant innocent unless proven guilty. And our suspicions, or, indeed, our prejudices we labor to put aside. *You* are under no such constraint.

CHARLES: I am a medical man. My oath . . .

ATTORNEY: Yes. Your oath obligates you to the patient.

CHARLES: . . . That's . . .

ATTORNEY: "Whatever I shall see or hear, in the course of my treatment . . . I . . ."

CHARLES: That's correct.

ATTORNEY: "I shall remain silent."

CHARLES: Yes. That's the Hippocratic oath.

ATTORNEY: Officers of the court. Are bound by oath, from acting upon prejudice. And schooled to reject the formation of opinions. And confine ourselves to facts. That is *our* oath. The Hippocratic oath, however, acknowledges that you *must* form opinions. You call them *diagnoses*. And adjures you only to keep them to *yourselves*. Is that correct?

(Pause.)

CHARLES: Yes.

ATTORNEY: Yes. Then you must have had opinions about those many cases in which you testified for the defense. That must be true. Mustn't it?

CHARLES: . . . Have had opinions?

ATTORNEY: As to the "actual" guilt or innocence of those for whom you testified.

CHARLES: My job was neither to indict nor acquit. But to understand their mental state.

ATTORNEY: But you must have thought some of them guilty.

CHARLES: That determination was the job of the courts.

ATTORNEY: Or, perhaps, to put it differently: You didn't care if they were guilty.

CHARLES: That's that's, yes, a less-attractive way of putting it. But, "*guilt*" . . .

ATTORNEY: . . . You didn't "care," or, more attractively, consider it your job. And had no scruples about testifying in support of those who, you may have thought actually guilty of crime.

CHARLES: My concern was not the alleged crime, but the defendant's mental state.

ATTORNEY: But some of them you must have believed guilty.

CHARLES: I believe that the Hippocratic oath debars me from answering that question.

ATTORNEY: Let me put it differently. Over the years. Would you consider it reasonable to assume that *some* of the cases in which a doctor had testified. On which, over the years, *you* had testified. Would it be reasonable, statistically to assume that some, as to whose mental state you testified, must have been legally guilty?

CHARLES: I . . .

ATTORNEY: Or: Is it logical to assume that all of the defendants brought to trial by the State, that every one of them, because of his mental state, should be adjudged not culpable?

CHARLES: I'm not a statistician.

ATTORNEY: Then are you going to sit there and tell me you believe that every case referred to you, that every patient on whose behalf you testified was morally innocent of the crime charged?

CHARLES: Their guilt or innocence was not my concern. It was my job to give, under oath, my opinions as to the defendant's mental state.

ATTORNEY: As you have said. And you did it, as we've said, for money: You were paid?

CHARLES: As . . .

ATTORNEY: Yes, "as is everyone here . . ." And you, put aside your prejudice, or say, suspicions as to their innocence or guilt.

CHARLES: Yes.

ATTORNEY: And never "made up your mind" as to their mental state until after you'd examined them.

CHARLES: That is correct.

ATTORNEY: Did you ever turn anyone down?

(Pause.)

We can subpoena your records.

CHARLES: The records are protected by law.

ATTORNEY: Perhaps, and perhaps not. Many people came to you. To ask you to speak for the defense. Did you ever turn anyone down?

CHARLES: My, my records . . .

ATTORNEY: It appears. You did *not*. In no case on record did you refuse a defendant's request to testify. In *no case*. For pay. Some of whom, at least, must, statistically, have been guilty of crime.

CHARLES: I did the job I was sworn to do. By my lights.

ATTORNEY: At that *time*.

CHARLES: Yes.

ATTORNEY: But you refused to testify *now*.

CHARLES: Yes.

ATTORNEY: Which is to say your understanding changed?

CHARLES: It is the case, I believe, that a man, as he ages, may increase in wisdom.

ATTORNEY: What has improved your understanding?

CHARLES: Time.

ATTORNEY: But not solely time. As many grow old, but we must allow few grow wise. Let me ask: Has *religion* improved your understanding?

CHARLES: Yes.

ATTORNEY: You came to religion late.

CHARLES: That's right.

ATTORNEY: Recently in fact.

CHARLES: Yes.

ATTORNEY: You were not always religious.

CHARLES: No.

ATTORNEY: Your parents were religious.

CHARLES: Yes.

ATTORNEY: And yet, for most of your life, you were not?

CHARLES: If you raise a child in the ways of the Lord, when he is young, he will not depart from them when he is old. As the rabbis said. But they do not say what he will do in between.

ATTORNEY: "If you raise a child in the Lord's Ways." That's in Proverbs.

CHARLES: Yes.

ATTORNEY: And have you returned to the Ways of the Lord? *Recently?* In your "age"? Is that correct?

CHARLES: I am attempting to.

ATTORNEY: What is it that prompted you?

CHARLES: Are my religious beliefs not . . .

ATTORNEY: Why *now*?

CHARLES: I . . .

ATTORNEY: At the same time as the alleged . . .

CHARLES: I don't know.

ATTORNEY: The alleged crimes of the young man.

CHARLES: I . . .

ATTORNEY: Who was your patient. You turned to religion. Why now?

CHARLES: I'm trying. To live in accordance with the dictates of the Bible.

ATTORNEY: Do you feel that they supercede your responsibilities as a citizen?

CHARLES: The two are not mutually exclusive.

ATTORNEY: Where you feel they are in conflict, how will you choose between them?

CHARLES: I have a conscience.

ATTORNEY: And that conscience comes from where? Does it come from God?

CHARLES: I believe it does.

ATTORNEY: And *does* that conscience always speak with clarity?

CHARLES: One, being human, and of other-than-divine understanding . . . One sometimes *requires* guidance.

ATTORNEY: Where is the guidance found?

CHARLES: It may be found in *meditation*, in *study*, in *prayer*.

ATTORNEY: May it be found in the Bible?

CHARLES: Yes.

ATTORNEY: And is that what you've discovered, in your return to religion?

CHARLES: I was traumatized. By the boy's crime. *You* appreciate that. For all your "performance." I know you do. And *I* sought some understanding.

ATTORNEY: What did you come to understand?

CHARLES: That there is a plan. That the plan is unknowable. That we are part of the plan.

ATTORNEY: Do you believe the Bible is the Word of God?

CHARLES: I believe that, written by the Hand of God, *or* Moses, or by those they inspired, the Bible contains divine wisdom.

ATTORNEY: Would you set yourself up to deny the Word of God?

CHARLES: I fervently pray that I would not.

ATTORNEY: The martyrs. Suffered fire and sword rather than denounce what they understood as God's Will.

CHARLES: That's right.

ATTORNEY: What have you elected *you're* prepared to suffer? To defend God's Word?

CHARLES: I pray.

ATTORNEY: Yes. That?

CHARLES: That, I, I don't know the answer to your question. I pray, only, for strength to abide by my conscience.

ATTORNEY: And if that bid you go against the laws of the State?

CHARLES: I believe that's called "religious freedom."

ATTORNEY: I will offer evidence that you have never refused to testify for a defendant in a court of law. NEVER REFUSED TO SUPPORT A CLAIM OF INNO-CENCE OR OF MITIGATION. By reason of mental or emotional incompetence. Yet. Now. For the *first time*. In a long career. You have refused such employment. You've testified that should you form an opinion, of a patient's guilt, you never act on it. And yet, you, finally, have turned a patient down. A man under your care accused of a crime. Will you say why?

CHARLES: I reread the Hippocratic oath.

ATTORNEY: What caused you to reread the oath?

CHARLES: My studies.

ATTORNEY: Your studies in religion.

CHARLES: All right, yes.

ATTORNEY: But surely the oath had been before you constantly.

CHARLES: I read it with new understanding.

ATTORNEY: Because you found religion.

CHARLES: Yes.

ATTORNEY: So you rejected the young man's plea, then, for religious reasons?

CHARLES: If you will.

ATTORNEY: No, that's what you just testified. That there is a "higher law." That, in confusion, we must refer to it, and that it is found in the Bible.

CHARLES: If you will.

ATTORNEY: Permit me. "You shall not pervert justice." You recognize the quotation?

CHARLES: Yes. It's in Leviticus.

ATTORNEY: And you say it's the Word of God.

CHARLES: I do.

ATTORNEY: And several pages later, in Leviticus, we find: "A man who lies with another man, as with a woman, has committed an abomination. He shall be put to death."

CHARLES: Yes?

ATTORNEY: "A man . . ."

CHARLES: I heard you.

ATTORNEY: Is that familiar to you?

CHARLES: Yes.

ATTORNEY: Is it the Word of God?

CHARLES: It's in the Bible.

ATTORNEY: Do you believe it? Do you or don't you?

CHARLES: No. I don't.

ATTORNEY: You don't.

CHARLES: No.

ATTORNEY: *Although* it's in the Bible.

(*Pause.*)

CHARLES: No.

ATTORNEY: Do you consider homosexuality a sin?

CHARLES: I do not.

ATTORNEY: But yet it's in the Bible. Do you believe in the laws of the Bible?

CHARLES: The laws, as any laws require . . .

ATTORNEY: Do you . . .

CHARLES: Re . . . They require interpretation. That's why there are judges.

ATTORNEY: "A practicing homosexual must be killed." That's open to interpretation?

CHARLES: Of course.

ATTORNEY: Interpret it for me.

(Pause.)

CHARLES: I'd have to . . .

ATTORNEY: You don't have an answer?

CHARLES: I would have to . . .

ATTORNEY: Yes?

CHARLES: I would have to consult a rabbinical . . .

ATTORNEY: Prior to that consultation. How have *you* acted upon that biblical law?

CHARLES: I haven't acted upon it.

ATTORNEY: But yet you know of it.

CHARLES: Yes.

ATTORNEY: Did it affect your thinking?

CHARLES: No.

ATTORNEY: It meant nothing to you.

CHARLES: That's right.

ATTORNEY: So we may say you were "unmoved." May we say that? "Unmoved." At the situation of those not only scorned but put in peril by the book to the dictates of which you ascribe your behavior. The Bible, which, "uninterpreted," as you say, licenses, as we speak, the abuse, indeed, the murder of citizens because of sexual preference.

(Pause.)

Is homosexuality a crime?

CHARLES: No.

ATTORNEY: Is it an "abomination"?

(Pause.)

CHARLES: No.

ATTORNEY: Then why have you refused to testify, IN THE SOLE CASE IN WHICH YOU HAVE, IN ALL YOUR YEARS, REFUSED TO TESTIFY? —And after your astounding religious conversion—in support of a patient under your care? I await your response.

SCENE 7

Charles, sitting. Richard enters with a file folder.

CHARLES: . . . *All right* . . .

    (Richard hands Charles a letter.)

RICHARD: You've been summoned to appear before the Licensing Board.

CHARLES *(Reading)*: "Unprofessional conduct . . . reflecting discredit upon . . ."

RICHARD: I'm sorry.

CHARLES: That's their job.

RICHARD: *That's* gracious.

CHARLES: What's the alternative? To go mad?

RICHARD *(Referring to the letter)*: Do you want someone in the office to attend you? It's not my line of expertise, of course, you should have someone who *does* it. But if . . .

CHARLES: I don't know if they allow counsel.

RICHARD: I don't know either. It says here they're going to require your files.

CHARLES: I don't care what they say. I'm done.

RICHARD (*Simultaneously*): You're done practicing . . .

CHARLES (*Simultaneously*): The entire thing is a sham. Who have I, I've helped *no* one; *none* of us help anyone. *I* couldn't help the boy. It's a loathsome business. I've been making my living at it; and what has it caused but misery? The State wants to intervene, let *them* intervene. Is it *my* job: to say who's sane? Who's *insane*? The boy? Killed ten people, and they're trying *me*? And that's called RATIONAL? For the love of God. I'm done.

(He puts the file folder on the desk.)

These are the boy's records.

RICHARD: Why do you want me to have them?

CHARLES: Because I lack the courage to destroy them. Could they force you to surrender them?

RICHARD: The parallel may be the old law school test: the criminal comes to seek counsel. And he places a gun on the desk. Which he may have used to commit a crime.

CHARLES: And what are you bound to do?

RICHARD: How is Kath?

CHARLES: You can't answer my question?

RICHARD: I'll have to think about it.

CHARLES: I haven't committed a crime.

RICHARD: Of course not.

CHARLES: So, if I give you the files . . .

RICHARD: You should surrender them, Charles.

CHARLES: I won't do it.

RICHARD: Is that wise?

CHARLES: I don't know, but it's my decision. I'm giving them to you. To hold. And ask you not to read them.

RICHARD: Are those your instructions?

CHARLES: Yes.

RICHARD: I'm your attorney. And I'll follow your instructions.

(Pause.)

CHARLES: You must think I'm a fool.

RICHARD: I think you've been shocked. And humiliated. That there's no way you can think clearly. It's time to let the law work. And obey the law.

CHARLES: I should destroy them. But that would be against the law.

RICHARD: That's correct.

CHARLES: But I won't "give them up."

RICHARD: Will you tell me why?

CHARLES: Because it's immoral. Because I'm being coerced. Into an act I find repugnant. And to submit because of the threats. Of the State. Is cowardice. That the *Board* wants to discredit me, this is the answer to your question, does not release me from my oath.

RICHARD: They'll take your license.

CHARLES: I'm giving it up anyway. I'm done.

SCENE 8

Kath is sitting at a small table. She wears a hospital gown. Charles enters. Pause.

CHARLES: How are you?
KATH: Oh. Is that what one says?
CHARLES: I don't know what one says.
KATH: But you've been here before.
CHARLES: Not here.
KATH: Places like this.
CHARLES: But not with you.
KATH: That's right.

(Pause.)

CHARLES: What can I bring you?
KATH: No. No. They told you. You can't bring me anything here.

CHARLES: That's right.

(*Pause.*)

KATH: How is the case going?

CHARLES: The case is not important. You're important.

KATH: The case is important to you.

CHARLES: But it's not important to us.

KATH: Yes. It is.

CHARLES: All that's important is you.

KATH: I don't think I'm worth it.

CHARLES: I know. But you are.

(*Pause.*)

How are you?

KATH: I'm so frightened.

CHARLES: I know.

KATH: I don't know who I am.

CHARLES: You're my wife. I love you. And I put you under impossible strain.

KATH: Perhaps you were doing what you thought was right.

CHARLES: Thank you. I thank you. But I don't *know* it was right. If . . .

(*Pause.*)

If the price of my . . . *dilemma* . . .

KATH: Yes.

CHARLES: Was finding you here.

KATH: Then perhaps this is part of your "punishment"?

CHARLES: I don't know.

KATH: But here I am.

CHARLES: You *broke*. Everyone . . . Has his breaking point. And I've always marveled. Since I met you. At your *goodness*. I've put you. In an impossible place. And I think your . . . your *break* came from, in part, from . . .

KATH: I . . .

CHARLES: Your inability to care for me.

KATH: Is that what you think?

CHARLES: Yes.

KATH: I have to go back soon.

CHARLES: I love you, Kath.

KATH: Thank you.

CHARLES: Stay for a while.

KATH: They have to *check* on you. They . . .

CHARLES: I know.

KATH: To check you in.

(*Pause.*)

Every quarter-hour.

CHARLES: How are you doing?

KATH: It's hard.

CHARLES: What could I do to make it easier?

KATH: I don't know.

CHARLES: Is it difficult for you, my coming?

(*Pause.*)

They said they'd give us a pass. Tomorrow, if you like. We could go off the grounds. What do you think?

KATH: I'd rather stay here.

CHARLES: All right.

KATH: Have you looked at my reports?

CHARLES: No.

KATH: You haven't?

CHARLES: No, of course not. And they wouldn't show them to
me.
KATH: They wouldn't?
CHARLES: No.
KATH: But you're a doctor.
CHARLES: But I'm not *your* doctor.

(Pause.)

Kath? How are you, Kath?
KATH: Not good. They'll come by in a bit.
CHARLES: I know.
KATH: Of course you know.

(Pause.)

I couldn't take it.
CHARLES: No, I understand.
KATH: No, you don't.
CHARLES: All right. I'm glad you're safe.
KATH: I'm not safe.
CHARLES: Are you going to try it again?
KATH: I don't know.
CHARLES: Well, in any case, you're safe from that.
KATH: Yes. That's the problem.
CHARLES: The *situation*. Will pass.
KATH: That's not the problem.
CHARLES: Then, what is the problem?
KATH: I can't tell you.
CHARLES: Then, how can I help you?
KATH: You can't help me. Did you look at the charts?
CHARLES: No. I told you.
KATH: But you might have lied. People lie. You know that.
Everyone lies. *Doctors* certainly lie. The *boy* lied.

(Pause.
　　She rises.)

CHARLES: Talk to me.

KATH: They said just a few minutes.

CHARLES: Talk to me.

KATH: I'll talk to you tomorrow.

CHARLES: I'll ask them to let me stay.

KATH: I'll talk to you tomorrow. With the doctor.

CHARLES: Talk to me now.

KATH: No. I want the doctors to be there.

CHARLES: Can you tell me why?

KATH: So I can be safe.

CHARLES: What can't you tell me? After all this time.

(Pause.)

KATH: I had an affair.

CHARLES: Is that why you're here?

(Pause.)

Kath. You had an affair.

KATH: Yes.

CHARLES: With whom?

KATH: With Richard.

(Pause.)

CHARLES: How long did it go on?

KATH: Some time.

CHARLES: I see.

(Pause.)

Is it over?

KATH: Yes.

CHARLES: Well, then, it's done.

(Pause.)

KATH: I have to go.

(Kath rises and knocks on the door.)

You used to tell me I'm "some girl."

CHARLES: You're my girl.

KATH: I'm not a girl.

CHARLES: That's how I think of you.

KATH: But that's not what I am.

CHARLES: I understand.

KATH: What do you understand?

CHARLES: That you . . .

KATH: All right.

CHARLES: . . . were under intolerable stress . . .

KATH: . . . All right.

CHARLES: . . . that, in that state . . .

KATH: Yes.

CHARLES: He sed . . .

KATH: He didn't seduce . . .

CHARLES: Wait, that he, whatever *name* you want to . . .

KATH: Richard didn't seduce me.

CHARLES: No, I understand . . .

KATH: What do you understand?

CHARLES: That something "snapped."

KATH: Yes . . . ?

CHARLES: . . . That perhaps he offered you, a . . .

KATH: Yes?

CHARLES: A "haven" . . . I don't know—a *respite*, he . . .

KATH: Yes, that's right . . .

CHARLES: That, that, you need *love*. And that your love . . .

KATH: Go on.

CHARLES: That our love was, what, "thwarted." By the, the stress. Of our position. And when *this* occurred, and *that* occurred, then you took refuge. With someone with whom you could be free.

(Pause.)

And I don't begrudge you. Your affair. I'm not *angry* with you. I'm not going to *leave* you. In fact, I need to find *peace*. With you.

KATH: . . . To find peace.

CHARLES: And ask your forgiveness. And thank *you*.

KATH: . . . Thank me . . . ?

CHARLES: For staying with me. *All* this time. When *I* was struggling.

KATH: You were struggling?

CHARLES: With *this*. With. My "practice." With, with my "profession." I couldn't help the boy, I could help *no* one, I couldn't help *you*. Whom did I aid? With what "knowledge"? They're right. And I took money. To "listen." To do *nothing*. They're right.

KATH: . . . Yes . . . ?

CHARLES: . . . And I knew it was a sham. And. Whatever misfortune, I've encountered. *And* brought upon you. I understand it. It came from a sinful, vile hypocrisy. And pride on my part. Which led to this. Of course it did..

KATH: And you say *you're* at fault.

CHARLES: I am.

KATH: When did you realize it?

CHARLES: You know when I did.

KATH: Tell me.

CHARLES: When the boy. *Shot* those people. When I read his *ravings*.

(Pause.)

When . . .

KATH: And what did you do?

CHARLES: I confessed myself before God. And pleaded for mercy.

KATH: And your prayers were answered?

CHARLES: They were "heard." Which is more than I deserve.

KATH: And so you found the answer in God.

CHARLES: That's right. I don't ask you to believe it. Or to accept it. But . . .

KATH: . . . But?

CHARLES: My God, we were involved in a *tragedy*, the State argues that his act was rational, the Defense wants me to explain why he should be excused.

KATH: No, we couldn't excuse him.

CHARLES: I couldn't. Or myself. For participating in the farce. That somehow I could help him.

KATH: And so you refused to testify.

CHARLES: That's right.

KATH: At whatever the cost.

CHARLES: That's right.

KATH: As a sort of penance . . .

CHARLES: As a moral choice.

KATH: And how did you arrive at your choice?

CHARLES: I prayed.

KATH: And your prayers were answered.

CHARLES: I believe they were.

KATH: Then, you must be a good man.

CHARLES: I would like to be.

KATH: And came here to profess your love to a bad woman.
CHARLES: I don't believe you're bad.
KATH: . . . No . . .
CHARLES: I believe. You were driven.

(Pause.)

KATH: I think about him.
CHARLES: But it's over. Is it over?
KATH: Oh yes.
CHARLES: Then, you don't need to tell me anything more.
KATH: Do you love me that much?
CHARLES: I do.
KATH: And what will happen now?
CHARLES: You'll come back, and . . .
KATH: You'd "take me back."
CHARLES: Of course.
KATH: And "forgive me"?
CHARLES: Yes. I will.
KATH: And if I don't want to come back?

(Pause.)

CHARLES: Do you want to go to Richard?
KATH: I can't.
CHARLES: Why not?
KATH: Because he respects his family.

(Pause.)

And he. Would not *expose* them. To the shame. To which you have, so easily, exposed me. Did you think of me? For *one moment*? When you "found religion"? When you "changed your life"? And was I supposed to put on a fuck-ing *veil*, and walk *behind* you? Meekly. While our friends left, while your patients left and the world turned on you, while they took your *license*? And the one man, I could turn to. For comfort? *Comforted* me. As long as he could. And when he could not . . .

CHARLES: I understand.

KATH: You understand what?

CHARLES: That people can die of a broken heart.

KATH: Yes. That's right.

CHARLES: And I understand how one may heal it.

KATH: How is that?

CHARLES: By turning to God.

KATH: When did you turn to God?

CHARLES: When I had nothing.

KATH: Yes. When things became so bad that you had nothing. And wanted to die.

CHARLES: The boy wrote that I hated him. Because I "wouldn't help him." But I tried to help him.

KATH: Yes, of course you did.

CHARLES: . . . According to my understanding. And I failed.

(Pause.)

After the murders? I was *set* upon.

KATH: Yes. You were.

CHARLES: And I turned to God. For wisdom, Kath. Because I didn't understand. Why I was being punished. Why was I being punished?

KATH: Are you asking me?

CHARLES: Why in the name of God am I being punished?

KATH: Because you gave the boy back the gun.

(Pause.)

You gave him back the gun. It's in your files. Richard told me. The boy brought the gun into the office. And he told you what he planned to do. And at the end of the hour you said, "That's all we have time for today." And he took the gun and killed those people. It's in your notes.

(Pause.)

Richard, you know, he always loved me. We were going to go away. But when he read the files. When he learned what you did, how could he stay with me? Because it *would* come out. *You* know that. I understood. It was not only him, but his children. And his family, whose name would then forever be linked with ours. With the name of a monster. And he just couldn't do it. I understood. But it broke his heart. It broke his heart.

(Pause.)

And, so, you've killed us all. You good, good man.

END

DAVID MAMET's numerous plays include *Oleanna*, *Glengarry Glen Ross* (winner of the Pulitzer Prize and New York Drama Critics' Circle Award), *American Buffalo*, *Speed-the-Plow*, *Boston Marriage*, *November*, *The Anarchist* and *Race*. He wrote the screenplays for *The Verdict*, *The Untouchables* and *Wag the Dog*, and has twice been nominated for an Academy Award. He has written and directed ten films, including *Homicide*, *The Spanish Prisoner*, *State and Main*, *House of Games*, *Spartan* and *Redbelt*. In addition, he wrote the novels *The Village*, *The Old Religion*, *Wilson* and many books of nonfiction, including *Bambi vs. Godzilla: On the Nature, Purpose and Practice of the Movie Business*; *Theatre*; *Three Uses of the Knife: On the Nature and Purpose of Drama* and the *New York Times* bestseller *The Secret Knowledge: On the Dismantling of American Culture*. His HBO film *Phil Spector*, starring Al Pacino and Helen Mirren, aired in 2013. He was co-creator and executive producer of the CBS television show *The Unit*. His novel *Chicago* was published in 2018. He is a founding member of the Atlantic Theater Company.